Chicken Soup for the Soul®

The Beautiful Game

D0308242

Chicken Soup for the Soul: The Beautiful Game
Inside World Soccer's Greatest Cup Competition
Published by Chicken Soup for the Soul Publishing, LLC www.chickensoup.com

The publisher gratefully acknowledges the many publishers and individuals who
granted Chicken Soup for the Soul permission to reprint the cited material.

Artwork courtesy of Alexandra McGrath.

This commemorative edition was sponsored and compiled by CertainRate Inc.
ISBN 978-0-692-23408-2

24 23 22 21 20 19 18 17 16 15 14   01 02 03 04 05 06 07 08 09 10 11

The Beautiful Game

Inside World Soccer's
Greatest Cup Competition

Chicken Soup for the Soul Publishing, LLC
Cos Cob, CT

Chicken Soup *for the* Soul

www.chickensoup.com

Contents

Becoming a Leader

by Carlos Bocanegra

rowing up, I always had dreams of being successful, but I didn't know exactly what I wanted to be. Over time, I grew to love sports, and I became a professional athlete through hard work and dedication. Having been a professional soccer player now for more than fourteen years, I can look back on many proud moments. I made my professional debut for Major League Soccer's Chicago Fire in 2000, and since then I have been fortunate to represent a number of great clubs, both in the United States and Europe, including England, Scotland, France, and Spain.

Throughout my career, I have interacted with people from all walks of life, both on and off the pitch. It truly made me realize that, without a doubt, soccer is the global game. The FIFA World Cup is the ultimate culmination of this, and I have been fortunate to participate in two of these momentous events.

My international career began in 2001 when I made my debut against South Korea. When I first joined up with the U.S. Men's National Team (USMNT), I made a point of watching established players like Claudio Reyna, Brian McBride, and Eddie Lewis. I saw how they carried themselves on and off the field, and how they went about training. At the time, I don't really think it sunk in, but these guys taught me a great deal about soccer, leadership, and personal growth.

I will never forget my first game as captain against China on June 2, 2007. It was a warm-up game for the CONCACAF Gold Cup, which we went on to win later that summer. It was very special for me because the game was in San Jose, and my whole family was able to be there. Not only was representing the United States an unforgettable feeling, but doing so as captain made the entire experience even more special. I learned that things are not always going to go as you'd hoped, but being optimistic and building team character can go a long way. We must accept that mistakes will be made, but by leading by example and encouraging other team members to do their best, we can be proud of our team regardless of the final result.

Every captain is different, and each brings his own set of skills and qualities. My strongest quality has always been my positive energy. I have always tried to spread encouragement throughout my team, and I tend to look on the bright side of life instead of focusing on the negatives.

In 2006, it was difficult to go out in the group stages in Germany. It still brings a very unpleasant taste to my mouth when I think of it. As captain in 2010, I knew we had been given a chance to make up for this defeat, and I wanted to do all I could to help the team progress in South Africa. I wanted to be part of a team remembered for doing something special in the largest sporting event in the world. It wasn't easy going into that World Cup knowing that our first game was going to be against a very highly rated England side. Walking out of the tunnel against England in that first game of the World Cup is still a very vivid memory for me because the game had been so hyped up on both sides of the Atlantic. I felt a lot of nervous energy taking those steps toward the field, but I was so excited. These are the moments you live for as a soccer player.

When we ended up drawing that match 1–1, it felt like we could have run through a wall with our energy. That feeling, that buzz, will always stand out in my mind. For me, it was a crucial game because we were able to demonstrate our value as a team, both to our fans and to ourselves. It gave us the momentum to continue believing that we could do better and built the way for us to go through the group stage in first place for the first time in our country's history.

I was most proud of the U.S. team in 2010 because, above all, we knew we needed to work together, share responsibilities, and make personal sacrifices in order to make our collective strength greater than if we had only applied our individual talents. We did just that and became the best team we could be.

As much as I remember the 2010 World Cup in South Africa for our success on the pitch, I will also never forget the friendships and relationships that were formed. The World Cup is such a big event, and we had a fantastic group of guys. I formed many lasting friendships that have stayed with me today. By nature, the USMNT is a very diverse group with players coming from different states, backgrounds, and nationalities. It was a huge honor and privilege to put such a group together. We shared many cool moments together, which I will never forget for the rest of my life.

As my professional career comes to an end, I look forward to spending a little more quality time with my family. Hopefully, I can apply some of the leadership lessons I have learned to help my kids grow up and make their dreams come true—just as I managed to do with mine.

Undefeated Underdogs

by Andy Boyens

t was November 14, 2009, and the tension of 35,000 New Zealanders hung thick in The Cake Tin (Westpac Stadium). The players had a strong taste of South Africa 2010 in their mouths, but only one team would enjoy the honour of representing their country at the FIFA World Cup. For New Zealand, it would be only their second appearance at the World Cup Finals. For Bahrain, it would be their first. Neither team could have wanted it more.

I was privileged to be part of the All Whites team that night. It is, hands down, the best footballing memory I have. Not just because we were victorious. Not just because it meant we had qualified for the World Cup. It was because we were able to share the experience with a nation that lived through it with us on home soil. The noise at Westpac Stadium that night was like nothing I'd ever experienced on a football pitch. Perhaps the most satisfying part of all was that no one (apart from ourselves and our country) thought we had a chance.

There is always one group at the World Cup that is termed the "group of death." We didn't have to wait for the draw to know that whatever group we were drawn in would be a group of death for us. We had a great team—a mixture of experience and youth who all seemed to be peaking at the right time. But we were also the only team to be going to the World Cup with amateur players on our roster. They worked nine-to-five jobs and managed to fit football into their busy schedules around work and family. The majority of our players played outside the top leagues in the world, and I'm pretty sure the collective salary of our players could have been matched by an individual on most other teams going to the World Cup. It was easy to say (and was said on numerous occasions by many sources) that New Zealand was just making up the numbers in South Africa. Having said all that, Kiwis are a special breed, a resilient bunch. We love a challenge, and there was an inherent belief within the squad that, while qualifying for the World Cup was a massive achievement, we still had a few more heads to turn.

I remember very clearly our country name being read out in Group F. I was sitting at home with my wife. I usually go on the assumption that my wife knows nothing about football. However, she surprised me that day when she turned to me, laughed out loud, and said very sarcastically, "Oh, that's not too bad, babe. You only have to play the World Champions."

We were grouped with Italy, Paraguay and Slovakia—huge teams in world football with world-class players. It was daunting and exciting all at the same time.

Royal Bafokeng Stadium, Rustenburg, was the setting for our first game. Slovakia was ranked almost thirty places above us in the FIFA rankings. As we walked out onto the field before the match, we were greeted by a small but very noisy group of Kiwis. A few of the boys in the squad wandered over to say hello to the fans, and it was a great sight. In true NZ fashion, the supporters were dressed in full sheep costumes, and there were even a few Kiwi costumes floating around. The majority of the people we chatted to had made the trip to South Africa from New Zealand to cheer on the team. In the changing room before the game, we spoke about the commitment and sacrifices those supporters had made to be there. An entire country was backing us, and it was time to make them proud.

Slovakia probably had the better of the game and scored just after half-time to go one up. For whatever reason, however, they never really seemed too worried about pushing for a second. That's always a dangerous tactic. Despite our underdog status, we had an enormous belief in our squad, and we were determined to fight to the end. My memory of Winston Reid rising above the rest in the 93rd minute and planting a header in off the right post will stay with me forever. It was New Zealand's first-ever point in a World Cup and ended any feelings of doubt that were forced upon us by those who had written us off before the tournament. We were jubilant after the game, and even more focused and confident going into the biggest game of our lives.

Mbombela Stadium, Nelspruit, is an amazing venue. The roof is supported by eighteen giraffe-like towers in what is clearly a South African stadium. We were on a high, whilst our opponents, Italy—the World Champions at the time—had drawn their first game. The stadium was almost packed to the brim. As I looked around the changing room before the game, I'd never seen eleven players so up for a game in my life. The energy was contagious, and we took it into the opening minutes of the game, harassing the Italians and gaining good possession up the field. We won an early free kick, and our top marksman, Shane Smeltz, coolly slotted home after a slight defection fell to his feet. Little old NZ was leading the World Champions after ten minutes. Italy came at us with everything, but we held firm until a soft penalty was awarded to Italy in the 30th minute. On another day and with a different squad, things could have gone downhill from there, but we had an experienced team with great leaders throughout. The boys left everything on the field that day. And if Chris Wood's late strike from distance in the dying minutes had fallen a foot to the left, we would have taken an historic victory home with us that night. Instead, we earned a point off the champs and went into the last game in a position to progress to the next round.

Paraguay only needed a point to get through to the next round; we needed three. It was a bit of a chess match with neither team wanting to give up an early goal. As the second half rolled on, it was still nil all, and we just didn't have enough in the tank to push for the winner against a quality team like Paraguay.

In drawing the last game, we departed the tournament in third place in Group F, finishing above Italy. With Spain, the eventual winners, losing their first game, we became the only undefeated team at the tournament. World Cups are where dreams are made. For twenty-three blokes from New Zealand, we lived our dreams and forever etched our names in World Cup history.

They Think It's All Over...

by George Cohen

n the 1962 World Cup, Sir Alf (our manager) and England lost the first game against France. He realised there would have to be a lot of changes. He really only had five world-class players, so he spent the next three years building his team, or "family" as we called it.

In the build-up to the 1966 World Cup finals, England beat Portugal, West Germany, and Spain. We couldn't understand why we were 10–1 outsiders to win the Jules Rimet Trophy, but after our first game against Uruguay, the press felt that 10–1 was actually very good odds.

We drew the game as Uruguay had come with a ten-man defence, and we were more than happy with a draw. In the dressing room afterwards, Sir Alf looked us all squarely in the face and said, "Gentlemen, we were playing in front of 100,000 people and were expected to win. We haven't won, but we also haven't lost. Next time, you will be better, less anxious. Just concentrate on what you are doing."

I remember our third match against the French for one big incident—when Nobby Stiles fouled the French Captain Jacques Simon in front of the Royal Box.

Simon tried to "sell a dummy" to Nobby, who wasn't buying anything, and went straight through him. Simon went down like a stone, and I would say he was hit somewhere between the thyroid gland and his knee cap.

Nobby tried to disappear into the crowd of players that had congregated around the fallen Simon, and he hid behind me.

"What was that all about? What had he done to you?" I asked him.

"George, he called me Norbert," he said.

I explained, "Norbert is simply your name in French."

I still remember Nobby's shy look to this day, as if to say, "Oh, I'd better say sorry then!"

In the next match against Portugal, a very good side but one that relied very heavily on Eusébio, Sir Alf sat next to Nobby in the dressing room. He said, "Nobby, I need you to mark Eusébio out of the game."

Nobby replied, "Do you mean this game or the rest of his career?"

Sir Alf just smiled and said, "Do what is necessary."

Eusébio left the pitch in tears; it was a master class in marking.

In 1966 on our pre-World Cup tour of Scandanavia, Sir Alf told us, "What I told you, I echo now. You will not meet Brazil in the final." He was proven right because they were knocked out by Portugal, which played Argentina in their next match. This turned out to be the most unsavoury of football matches I have ever witnessed, ranging from terrible tackles to spitting in players' faces. Afterwards, Sir Alf called them "animals." Although he was made to apologise for this comment after our match with them, he refused to allow me to swap shirts with one of their players.

Everybody knows how England's match against Argentina unfolded, but I recall one humourous incident. As we were coming out of the tunnel at half-time, an Argentine player said to Nobby that he was going to "kick his teeth in." The already toothless Nobby's reply was succinct: "You'll have a tough job. They are in the dressing room."

Fate again played a hand when Jimmy Greaves, our starting forward, injured his lower shin in the French match and was unable to play. Sir Alf brought in Geoff Hurst to play up front. He played so well that although Greaves was passed fit for the next match, Sir Alf decided to stay with Geoff. The rest is history!

The 1966 World Cup final against West Germany at Wembley was an unbelievable experience for me. Once again, fate played a hand in my professional life as the two previous England right backs, Jimmy Armfield and Ken Shellito, were injured, and Sir Alf gave me my opportunity. I grasped it with both hands.

I honestly believed that we would beat West Germany. Many people thought the West German side was superior, but I knew the heart of "our family" was far greater than theirs. It also helped that we were very familiar with the Wembley pitch. Not boggy but soft, the grass tufts meant players ran two yards slower, but the ball went one yard faster. No other team had this knowledge.

At the end of regular time with the game on a knife edge, Sir Alf pointed out that the Germans were "sold out" because of the pitch. Whilst they all collapsed, we remained standing to emphasise this point.

At the start of extra time, we very quickly emphasised our advantage and raised our game, but the Germans had nothing left. With the minutes ticking by and us winning 3–2, Bobby Moore chested the ball down. With Bobby Charlton shouting at him to play the ball into the crowd, he sprayed a magnificent thirty-yard pass to Geoff, who took it in his stride and blasted the ball into the back of the net. What a way to score a hat trick in a World Cup final. World champions in our home country!

As we sat in the dressing room trying to comprehend what had just happened, I remember a knock on the door. A Football Association official entered and advised us that we had been awarded £22,000. I thought I was a millionaire until it was explained that we had to share it among all of us. After taxes, I received £634 for winning the World Cup, whilst the Germans were given cars and villas. Oh, how the world has changed!

Later at a reception, Harold Wilson, the then Prime Minister, explained to me that the euphoria of winning the World Cup had boosted the whole of England, and that we had saved the pound from being down valued (well, at least for sixteen months). Amazing!

My team members and I still meet as often as possible as we are all still great friends. "The family" has lost several members, but our spirit has never been broken.

Winning the 1966 World Cup taught me that it is not just ability that can win the game. You also need belief, desire, team spirit, humour—and it always helps if fate decides to play a part.

The Englishman and the Mariachi Band

by Tony Collins

It was 1965 when Dad, a milkman at the time, helped to start the most memorable period of my life. One of his customers was Sir Stanley Rous, who was President of FIFA, and Dad asked him, more through cheek than any real expectation, if there was any chance of procuring tickets for him and his son for any of the World Cup matches the following year, which was being held in the football motherland: England.

To Pop's amazement, Rous arranged tickets for us for all ten games: nine at Wembley Stadium and one at the ancient White City stadium, which was the original Olympic stadium from 1908.

I remember Portugal going into this tournament as big favourites, with the genius of Eusébio fronting their attack. Nobody expected England to really do anything, especially after their first result, a 0–0 draw with Uruguay. We were just happy to be there and hosting the event!

I remember qualifying for the quarter-finals where we played Argentina. It was a horribly bad-tempered game, and Rattan was sent off for La Albiceleste. All I really remember was him refusing to leave the field of play after his dismissal—something that shocked us well-mannered and rule-abiding Brits!

England then played the favourites, Portugal, in the semi-final and we won, allowing us to play the fearsome West Germans in the final.

By this time, we were now fully convinced that England would lift the World Cup, and it was completely against the fairytale's script when West Germany scored. But we recovered and went 2–1 ahead until a last-second equaliser by West Germany. However, England persevered, and when the fourth goal went in, we all realised we had won it.

Apart from the great honour of being at all of these matches, the other thing I remember clearly was that there were so many people from different countries. Everyone was so friendly, and there was absolutely no trouble whatsoever.

After the final, Dad and I travelled home. When we left Turnham Green underground station, adorned in our England scarves and bobble hats, to our lump-in-throat amazement, people applauded us as we walked along High Street as if we had won it ourselves.

When we arrived home, the neighbours applauded us, too. It was the most surreal experience of my life. It still sends chills down my spine when I recollect those moments, as if I wasn't emotional enough at the time. I was just seventeen years old, but I promised myself that I had to experience the next World Cup.

I started saving £2 from my weekly salary of £10 for the next four years. This enabled me to pay the £250 fee to the England Supporters Club for flights, accommodations, and tickets in Mexico.

I remember feeling a sense of surrealism that I was going to Mexico. It was a place you only saw in films, and at that time it was unheard of for us ordinary folk to fly across the Atlantic, especially to watch a football match!

In Mexico, we were privileged to stay with a Mexican family rather than in a hotel. Although I had chosen this option because it was the cheapest, it turned out to be the most fantastic experience. It was also when I first started speaking Spanish.

One of our party was good, old Harold Moss. He was about seventy at the time, but he knew everyone in football. We were introduced to Alf Ramsey, the England Manager, and most of the England players at the training ground. We also met Lord Harlech, who was the Queen's cousin, and most of the journalists of the day.

When England qualified for the quarter-finals, which was played in León, we were told that it was a complete sell-out and there was no way for us to get tickets. Our hearts sank. We had come all this way, and we were going to miss seeing our team play in the quarters. However, Lady Luck decided it wasn't quite time to stop shining down on us as she presented us with the father of the family we were staying with. He had a friend from Peru who told him there were hundreds of Peruvian supporters with tickets for England's game in Guadalajara, but they were desperate to get tickets for Peru's match—tickets that we had!

We drove halfway to León in a hired car to a cantina in the middle of nowhere in the Mexican High Sierra, where there were literally hundreds of Peruvians. We shook hands, swapped tickets, and headed off to our respective matches. Them against Brazil; us against West Germany, again.

Our game started so well. We went 2–0 up and were cruising, but as history will tell you, we ended up losing 3–2. I have never felt such a feeling of desolation. We had the game in our grasp, but we threw it away. It is a feeling that is now all too familiar to England fans.

The atmosphere was magnificent, but nothing could raise my spirits—or so I thought. When we arrived back at our home away from home, the family had arranged for a mariachi band to greet us. The tequila flowed freely, and to be perfectly honest, I don't remember much more, but the pain had definitely started to dull.

After that, we went to Mexico City, where we saw Italy beat West Germany 4–3. Three days later, we went to see Brazil versus Italy in the final.

I still pinch myself when reminiscing about myself as a young lad from England going all the way to magical Mexico and watching England play in the World Cup and then watching the World Cup final. I met so many good friends there and even came back to England with a young Mexican lady. But in case my wife is reading this story, I had better stop now!

A Shared Victory for All of the Azzurri

by Niccolo Conte

In the summer of 2006, as Italy and France were preparing to play the World Cup final, I had my face against the car window, searching for stray television screens through rain and restaurant windows as my Italian family of four drove through the unfamiliar streets of downtown Denver. Our summer drive from Dallas to Vancouver was in full swing, and our plans of arriving in Denver early, in time for the final, were dampened by a summer pouring, rivalled only by the rapid-fire Spanish radio commentary we were tuned in to. There was a restrained unrest between the four of us, as we'd already spent days together in the rouge Volvo station wagon driving across America, only stopping in the evenings to find a humble Best Western or La Quinta Inn to watch World Cup highlights of the Italian national team's trek across German stadiums. Our own trek toward a hotel for the night was progressing by inches, cars struggling through the streets that were flowing with rain.

As the radio commentary unfolded, we heard the starting whistle blow, the Berlin crowd cheer, and the celebratory starting line: "¡Y ahora, comienza la final, Italia, Francia!" As we crept past a restaurant, we spotted the glow of a television showing the final. My mother and father talked about stopping for dinner to watch, but were interrupted by the name of Zidane bellowed out in full force by the car's radio.

A flutter of French flags burst inside the restaurant as we listened to the long-held traditional cry of *"¡GOOOOOOAAAAAAL!"* It was promptly decided that we would find somewhere else to watch the final. Our search continued at a slow pace, and as the match played on, Zidane's name dominated the commentary. The Frenchman had given France the lead, and the sound of his name continuously raised the tension in the car as we were frozen in traffic, only able to listen to the rain and the commentary, *"¡Zidane con la pelota, Zidane se mueve bien, dribla torno a la defensa italiana, Zidane fuera del área, Zidane tira! Bien guardado, Zidane es muy peligroso para los italianos."* Just like we were powerless amidst the unmoving traffic, the Italian team was at the mercy of Zidane's feet.

Back then, I had a limited understanding of the Italian team and its composition. While I knew some names characterized by my father's comments ("Perrotta? In this team, he's about as useful as a hole in a dam"), I didn't know about the Azzurri and their staunch defence. I had no idea about their disciplined playing style, which was dictated by the cool-headed metronome that is Andrea Pirlo. My father had occasionally talked about how any of Italy's attacking developments were birthed in Pirlo's mind. It was his vision and execution that placed the ball onto Toni's statuesque head or Grosso's primed left foot. Back then, all I knew was that any little hope we had was tied to the laces of Pirlo's boot.

By now we had been driving around downtown Denver for more than an hour, and it was evident that there were no Best Westerns or La Quinta Inns around. As my parents decided to stop at the next hotel, we heard the Spanish commentary flare up: *"¡Pirlo está listo para tirar el córner, tira, Materazzi encabeza adentro! ¡Materazzi la torre, marca el gol para igualar!"* Pirlo had crafted a curled corner, placed with precision on Materazzi's head for the equalizer, and it was then that I saw the tower that was the Hyatt hotel. Once inside the pearly white lobby, I suddenly realized there wasn't a television showing the match in sight. The soft and languid tinkle of the lobby's self-playing piano was almost silent compared to the spitfire Spanish commentary in the car. To the calm and smiling attendants, our hurried Italian immigrant family looked like we had just reached salvation, only to despair that salvation's lobby was without football.

My sister's eyes were close to tears, continuously looking around at the pale walls in vain for a television as my parents checked in. She pulled at my father's jacket before the fearful words crept out, "What if they don't have any TVs...?" to which my father asked the attendant: "Do you have televisions in the rooms?" Her confused affirmation was enough to satisfy us. Bag porters stared as we hurriedly hauled our baggage up the stairs, with everyone in the family embracing my father's theory about elevators being too slow. Once inside the room, we lit up the large television in time for the second half. In the spacious, double-bedded room, our family piled into one bed, leaving space on the other bed for the luxurious room service dinner we had ordered.

It was there that I got my first true taste of football. I saw Zidane power through the Italian defence, only to be stopped by the acrobatic saves of Buffon. The Frenchman I feared so much was a blaze of unstoppable grace, and it was only his notorious headbutt that allowed my family and the rest of Italy to breathe. When it came time for penalties, all four of us lay unmoving on the bed, holding hands, until Fabio Grosso's winning penalty released our euphoria. The rushing of steps could be heard from the hallway as a lone Italian ran to the shared balcony, emptying his lungs into the nighttime rain with his love for the Azzurri. From the players on the field and the fans in the stadium, all the way to a stranger in the Hyatt and a family of four, Italy's victory brought us all a memory and joy that remains shared.

Now You Are a True Dutchman

by Joe Frederik

I've grown up knowing that, before I was born, "we, the Netherlands" lost two World Cup finals. In 1974, we got beaten by West Germany, and in 1978 by Argentina. The 1988 European Championship victory made up for it, but just a little bit. Germany's Gerd Müller and "Rensenbrink-hits-the-post" still haunted the nation. In 1978, Rob Rensenbrink hit the post in the 90th minute with a score of 1–1, sending the game into overtime. Never had we been so close to the World Cup trophy.

In 2010, the whole nation was ecstatic after we beat Brazil in the quarter-final. Brazil had been an obstacle during the 1994 World Cup (quarter-final) and the 1998 World Cup (semi-final), but we finally got our revenge. The Orange fever kicked in in the Netherlands. That fever really kicked in after the semi-final victory against Uruguay. We were going to the final. Could we finally get rid of our national tragedy by winning the final versus Spain and taking home the World Cup trophy for the first time?

July eleventh was the big day. The Museum Square in Amsterdam was filled with close to a million people. I was watching the match in a bar, nervous and restless. I couldn't sit still on my barstool, and I was living between hope and fear. It only got worse after the kick-off. The match was packed with emotions and tension, as if it radiated from the

TV. It was a real battle from the first minute. Five players were given a yellow card during the first half. Nigel de Jong's ridiculous studs-up kick to Xabi Alonso's chest was illustrative of the football fight that was going on in Johannesburg.

I was actually quite relieved during half-time. The score was still tied at 0–0, and we were still in the race to become the world champions. I was also relieved that Nigel de Jong was not sent off, although he should have been. But the most important thing during half-time was that I had fifteen minutes to calm down, cool off, and slow my heart rate.

It was already a hot day in the Netherlands, but in the jam-packed bar, the excitement of the match made the temperature go through the roof. I decided to take a short walk during half-time. I was not the only one. A lot of people took a quick walk, trying to lose that nervous feeling and wiping the anxiety sweat from their faces. As I walked back to the bar, I really hoped that the match would be decided during the second half because I didn't want an additional thirty minutes of tense overtime.

The second half started, and as I remember, it was a copy of the first half. The fight continued, and another four yellow cards were given. I started to lose hope a little bit because the Netherlands were not creating chances and ball possession was in Spain's favor. But then came the 62nd minute. Arjen Robben was put one-on-one with the Spanish goalie Iker Casillas by a pass from Wesley Sneijder. Robben's way to the goal seemed to take forever, and all I could think was: "What if he scores? Please let him score. Can you imagine if he scores? DO IT!" But he didn't. His effort touched Casillas' right foot, and the ball soared past the goal. I was in disbelief, with my hands on my head. I knew that if he scored, our team had the ability to protect the lead and take home the trophy.

I spent the rest of the second half hoping for another opportunity like that, but it never came. Luckily, Spain didn't create any opportunities either, so the match was sent into overtime.

There was no time for another walk outside; the match continued a couple of minutes after full-time. The overtime was no different from the first ninety minutes. Dutch defender John Heitinga received his second yellow card and was sent off in the second half of the overtime. A red card for a Dutch player was bound to happen, and Heitinga's sending off was an omen of what was about to come. Four minutes before the end of the game, Andrés Iniesta scored 0–1 to Spain. I knew immediately that this was the decisive goal, and that Spain would be the world champions. There was no way that Spain would allow the Netherlands to equalize in the remaining minutes.

I hated Spain and Andrés Iniesta at that moment, but I quickly made peace with the fact that we lost the final. We did not deserve to win, but at least we kept fighting (almost literally) till the bitter end. Maybe Iniesta just put us out of our misery or prevented a prolonged suffering because the Netherlands and penalty shoot-outs are not good friends.

I went outside to cool down a bit. As I sat on the sidewalk, an old man passed by and asked if I was upset about the lost final. He thought I looked sad. I said no, maybe a little. Of course, I would have preferred a different outcome, but it was what it was.

Then he told me that this was the best way to become a true Dutchman. "You have experienced a lost World Cup final, and you have experienced a 'Rensenbrink-hits-the-post' kind of moment with Arjen Robben's opportunity. Now you are a true Dutchman." It cheered me up because he really put the lost final into perspective. "It is what defines us as Dutch people," he said. "This is what we do. We create land out of water, and we lose World Cup finals. Have a good night and take care." He took off.

Just as I was about to get up and get back to the bar, I asked myself a question, one that I still ask myself today after four years: What if Robben...

The Neutral's Cup of Dreams

by Asit Ganguli

The entire concept of developing loyalties and rivalries out of nothing was witnessed firsthand in my own home in India. As an eight-year-old, I lay on the carpet, watching Argentina try to retain their title at the 1990 World Cup in Italy, against the might of the West Germans. As my brother and father supported the West Germans, I took my mother's side and stood for Argentina—a loyalty that I carry to this day. It was my loyalty for the Italians, and my brother and father's love for Brazil at the 1994 World Cup, which brought the Italian national team onto my fan radar.

Every four years, the biggest tournament in the world kicks off while one of the largest countries in the world has no choice but to watch the action unfold from afar. It might seem like a lonely place to be—sitting on the outside and looking in—but there is something special that happens every time the best in the world gather, and the rest sit aside.

The city of Kolkata in India is divided by a historical struggle every year as local football teams, East Bengal and Mohun Bagan, battle it out in one of the oldest and fiercest rivalries in the world. Streets and shops are either draped in the red-gold of East Bengal or the maroon-green of Mohun Bagan. The city is crazy about football, and these rivalries can get intense—almost riot-inducing.

However, every four years, every single individual puts aside his or her personal club rivalry and dons another hat—that of Argentina or Brazil!

The football-loving people of Kolkata have chosen their sides, and former rivals on the East Bengal-Mohun Bagan front—who probably wouldn't speak with each other or walk through the other's street—now brandish the same colours and sit side by side, sipping tea and watching their favourite Argentinean or Brazilian player weave his magic. The comments are still the same, as is the intensity. The difference, however, lies in the colours!

It is the beauty of colours that makes India such a "strange" country, for lack of a better word. You would imagine that in a place where there is no electricity, or barely six hours of electricity in a day, people would learn to develop simpler pleasures. Nothing, however, is simpler than watching some of the top players of the world fight it out on the pitch. In small towns and villages, where people have limited electricity supplied to their households, public demand dictates the time and duration of the power cut.

Small industries may remain powerless through the day, but come nighttime on a World Cup match day, there has to be non-stop supply during those two hours. For those two hours, as most of the village sits in darkness, one or two screens flicker in the odd home, where sits huddled the entire neighbourhood. Irrespective of who lives where or what kind of day they had, everyone flocks to that one house where the television set will run, showing these international football matches through satellite television that every single household has pooled-in to purchase.

The house hosting the match has no dearth of support either. People bring snacks, tea and food, ensuring there is a constant supply throughout the match. They do not understand a word of the commentary, nor do they understand the rules entirely. What they do understand is that the ball has to end up in the back of the net!

The advantage of being neutral and passionate about the sport is the incredible atmosphere that every single match creates, no matter what time of the day or night it might be. Neutral spectators, they say, have no side, but one look at these pubs and bars, and you would think otherwise. In India, we support both sides because we have no side! We do not have any loyalties to any of the teams, so even if two people are watching a game at home, chances are they will end up supporting different teams. That is the power of being neutral — the power to convert every single game into a lifelong rivalry. It doesn't take much to get us started — just a television set, the saved-up electricity, and some players kicking a ball about.

In a country where the sport struggles to find a foothold, such a response is surprising. However, one look at the world, and you realize instantly that this has nothing to do with the stature of the country on the world football-ladder. If passion were an adjudicator of global ranking in the sport, probably a hundred teams would be tied for first, and India would definitely be one of them.

The power of the World Cup brings people together. We sit under one roof, sipping tea, watching a game that we barely understand, and listening to commentary we do not comprehend. We set aside our daily worries, sitting late into the night, enjoying life for that brief moment when everything else stops, and all that matters is that the ball must end up in the back of the net.

The fact that India does not play in the World Cup has made absolutely no difference to the attention this competition gets. Forget the marketing and publicity gimmicks for a second, and look at what makes different people from all over the neighbourhood gather under one roof to watch a match.

Is it the publicity of the tournament?

Is it the magic of the marketing dollars spent in India?

Perhaps, it just has something to do with that ball hitting the net!

From Setbacks to Success

by Benny Jones

My story begins strangely not at the moment of triumph and unadulterated joy, but with the gut-wrenching disappointment that confirmed my passion for football and gave me my first real taste of its power over our emotions.

Wind the clock back ten years prior to glory. It is November 29, 1997. A young thirteen-year-old boy (me) stands among 80,000 Australian football fans at our national sports coliseum, the Melbourne Cricket Ground. The Socceroos lead 2–0 with fifteen minutes left to play after goals from Harry Kewell and Aurelio Vidmar. A win with any scoreline gets us through. We have Iran where we want them and one foot on the plane to France '98.

The atmosphere is electric, the anticipation palpable. The Socceroos' first World Cup finals appearance in twenty-four years is just fifteen minutes away. Iran scores. Never mind, we still lead. Before we can take a breath, they score again. Shock, confusion, anger. Full-time whistle goes. It finishes 2–2. We are eliminated on the away goals rule. You can hear a pin drop on the way home that night, as well as grown men weeping.

I cried that night. Maybe it was because so many others did likewise. But it felt confusing to draw a game, yet still lose. To realize something that we fleetingly considered "ours"—a berth in the World Cup—could be so easily taken away in fifteen mad, crazy minutes.

I've taken the long way round to arrive at my moment, though!

Fast-forward eight and a half years from that night (and another failed World Cup qualification campaign at the hands of Uruguay). It's June 12, 2006. We have qualified for the FIFA World Cup in Germany, ironically after sneaking past Uruguay, our opponents again, in a nail-biting penalty shoot-out the previous November.

I find myself in the beautiful German town of Kaiserslautern, making the long climb up the hill towards the Fritz-Walter-Stadion. Australia is playing Japan. It's the opening game for Group F (which also includes Croatia and a reasonably talented side from Brazil). It's hot—and I'm talking Australian summertime hot—but we love these conditions. Surely the Japanese won't.

I have travelled from afar to ensure I won't miss out on what I feel I was robbed of nine years earlier—a chance to witness Australian footballing history! The beer is flowing, although not cold for long. The bratwursts are plentiful. But all are sideshows to the main event. The football.

Kick-off, and for the first twenty-five minutes, both sides test each other out. If it's tough for us in the stands, it must be tough for the players running end to end in the searing heat. Then, out of nowhere, disaster—something we Socceroos fans have become all too accustomed to. Japanese midfielder Nakamura floats a hopeful ball into the Australian 18-yard box. Mark Schwarzer, our heroic, experienced keeper, is taken out of the play, and the ball rests in the back of our net. Twenty-thousand Australians, as well as eleven exasperated players on the pitch, yell "FREE KICK REFEREE" in unison. The referee is pointing back to the middle. Japan leads 1–0.

Half-time, no change to the score. Another beer to calm the nerves and some simmering frustration. A quick call back home to my father (it's 2:00 AM in Australia at the time), so little wonder I get the answering machine. No chance to vent there.

The second half gets underway, and despite Australia's best efforts and intentions, they are getting little reward. The clock ticks past 80 minutes, 81 minutes, 82 minutes… Time seems to be speeding up as we get closer to the finishing line. My head in my hands, all this distance, the financial sacrifices… Walking up that bloody steep hill pre-game, all for nothing!

In the 83rd minute, a long floated throw by Lucas Neill. The Japanese keeper flaps at it. There are bodies everywhere, ten yards out from the goal. Where's the ball? What? It's in the back of the net! We've scored! At this point, I have no idea who… but who bloody cares! We have just scored our first-ever goal in the World Cup finals! Beer is spilt; lungs are exploding. It's Tim Cahill, of course—the poster boy for our golden generation of stars.

Okay, now I've calmed down. What does this all mean? Well, at least we won't go home empty-handed. At least it's a draw, but better than the one I sat through back in 1997. The Socceroos are bombing on now as the Japanese begin to wilt in the heat. Yes! This was the plan all along. But Australian football and fairytales don't go hand in hand, so I'm anxious. Please don't let us concede later on.

Before I know it, it's that man Cahill again. He has the ball dead in front, twenty yards from the goal. Why is nobody closing him down? He rolls the ball under his foot once and sizes up his target. I know it's ridiculous as it doesn't literally happen, but it feels like, for that moment, time slows. The ball curls into the post. Oh no, surely not. Wait… it's deflected back across goal. What? It's in somehow, this beautiful round object has somehow found a way to cross the line. We lead 2–1. You can pinch me at this point. Surely I'm dreaming!

Cahill wheels away, mobbed by teammates and officials. I find myself handing out random hugs, and maybe a kiss or two. High-fives are being used in epidemic proportions. There's still time left, but we are on cloud nine now, and nothing can stop this green and gold juggernaut. Two minutes into injury time, John Aloisi leaves two Japanese defenders in his wake, and does what a good striker is paid to do! 3–1. Eight of the craziest minutes I've ever experienced as a sports fan. Period.

Aussie fans are singing… "We're top of Group F!" To be fair, neither Brazil nor Croatia had kicked a ball in anger yet. But we don't care. It's dreamland for long-suffering but loyal Australian football fans! I don't even remember the full-time whistle, but all I want to do is catch up with my pals outside the ground to relive it all again. One of them, Chris, is almost the first person I see outside the ground. No words. The cheesy grins on our faces say it all. We've done it. All those heartbreaks, disappointments and near misses. Worth it. For this one magical moment. For these eight magical minutes.

That's my story. I still occasionally relive those spine-tingling moments, and the effect never wears off. There is something mystical about a World Cup—win, lose or draw. The love of the game, the people from all walks of life. There's nothing to compare to it.

Boy, Was It Worth It

by Matt Leaver

I have played and watched football my entire life; in fact, football has *been* my entire life. Never, however, did I believe I would get to watch England at a World Cup live. It was just one of those events that I watched on TV or down at the pub with my friends. Never would it physically exist within my presence. That changed when Germany won the right to stage the 2006 World Cup, and I decided that would be the opportunity to make my dream come true.

Once the World Cup draw was made, the four of us—Graham, Charlie, Seb and myself—surfed the web, intimately studied all the maps, and excitedly organised the travel details. I could not quite accept that my dream was about to come true. This was the biggest *sporting* event—nay, the biggest *event* on the planet—and I was going to be a part of it.

On June 17, 2006, we awoke before dawn—although, to be honest, I hadn't slept a wink—and set off from our homes in the south of England on the two-and-a-half-hour journey to Dover to catch the ferry over to France. This journey was set in the glamorous surroundings of Graham's beat-up old banger. That was the plan anyway.

I should have realised then that things would not be as straightforward as we had planned. I had known these guys way too long to make that mistake. Graham, who had spent the evening prior in a much less-than-acceptable way than someone who had to arise before the next day's sun should, had overslept, and we simply could not wake him. This twenty-something man was eventually dragged out of bed and dressed by his good, old mum. However, despite setting and breaking numerous new land-speed records, we still missed the ferry and had to wait another two hours for the next one.

Once in France, we headed on the four-hour drive to Belgium. We arrived in Liège where we set up base in a local hotel. The night we arrived, Italy was playing, and there were a lot of Italians around. When they won, the streets were amass with Latin celebration—car horns, songs, whistles. The town was awash with joy. This made the anticipation of getting to Germany almost unbearable.

The next morning, we got the train to Cologne, Germany, leaving the car at the hotel in Belgium. She was starting to show her age, and we didn't want her to break down before we got to the game. When we arrived, we were greeted by thousands of England supporters around the town.

We spent the day drinking and patriotically singing along with other supporters and engaging in some banter with German fans as their team was playing during the day.

The moment we had been waiting for had come: the England game against Sweden. It was a great experience, and although it ended 2–2, the score meant that England had qualified in the group. I will not go into too much more detail, as the football itself was only the tip of the iceberg of the overall adventure.

Due to the late kick-off, we missed the train back to Liège and had to sleep on the hard waiting-room floor of the train station. We awoke in the morning, cold and stiff.

After we had returned home to England, the post-World Cup depression kicked in. It simply got to be too much, so we decided that we couldn't miss the next game. After speaking to many friends, two of us decided to travel back to Germany. Fortunately, Graham's brother had arranged to go two days later, so we managed to hitch a ride to the city of Gelsenkirchen—that's right, we were about to repeat the same journey across a continent!

We didn't have a hotel to stay in this time, so we left our car in a

29

car park and went to find the England supporters who were gathered in a square. We watched a German Elvis impersonator as entertainment — and, believe it or not, he was very good, although the alcohol may have affected our judgment.

We didn't have tickets for this game, so we watched it in a Rudelgucken, which was an area set up by local towns for fans of all nations to watch matches on big screens in each other's company. The atmosphere was indescribable, with not a hint of the projected trouble.

The usual England-knocked-out-in-the-quarter-finals-on-penalties-in-a-glorious-defeat predictably occurred, but this time it really hurt. Even worse, we had to sleep on a park bench as we couldn't find anywhere to stay. It was a long, sad journey home. It had taken us across four countries, cooped up like sardines in a ticking time bomb, but it was worth it!

The World Cup is a football tournament — it is *the* football tournament — but the football is, in fact, the least special thing about it. Granted, what occurs on the hallowed green stuff will always be able to reduce fully grown men to withering, sobbing shadows of their portrayed images, but the bonds you build with those around you during the ninety minutes, as well as the endless hours prior and post... well, those are the real moments. Dramatic though it may sound, the World Cup makes the world a better place, even just for a few weeks every four years. In the microcosm of the Rudelguckens, Iranians danced with Americans, the English sang with the Argentines, and the Croatians reconnected with their Serbian brothers. Now that is something special.

The Twelfth Man

by Eddie Lewis

A t 2:00 AM local time in Jeonju, South Korea, on June 17, 2002, my hands trembled, my eyes raced, and my sheets were soaked. Never before, nor since, have I ever been so unsettled before a game. The next day, USA faced off against Mexico, our staunch neighbor to the south. Relations were flat-out vengeful. The U.S. had been under the Mexican thumb for decades. But this American squad, this generation, was beginning to win the Border Battle. Leading up to the World Cup, the U.S. had notched consecutive and convincing wins over the Mexicans. Yet these victories received not more than a back-page blurb in the press. Maybe Sports Center mentioned it as they segued to commercial.

Tomorrow was different. For once, EVERYONE was watching. First-time American fans were in a fervor. The backyard brawl went global. When it mattered most, could we do it?

Big stages are very unforgiving. Heavily favored Olympic hurdlers crash out. Downhill skiers who have aced time trials crumble when the gates open for real. Super Bowl receivers suddenly suffer from butter fingers. Pressure has a way of breaking the backs of the strongest humans on the planet.

Would our backbones hold? We were the strongest eleven players representing a nation of nearly a billion. Could we stand tall and succeed while wearing the beloved red, white, and blue? It was time for American soccer to be acknowledged as a legitimate force. We were not a fluke. We were soldiers engaged in the battle of advancing our reputation, both domestically and abroad. We needed to clear a path for the advancement of future Americans coming up the ranks behind us.

The reason my linens were soaked was because this game was about more than me. I wasn't worried about how I would perform individually. I wasn't chasing a contract. I was chasing my own American dream. Patriotism kept me awake all night.

The next day, as I exited the stadium victorious, my hands again trembled and my eyes did race. After ninety minutes in the trenches, my jersey was soaked in sweet satisfaction. Not only did we win, but I played a role in the final goal of the game.

I am a player known for assisting goals, not scoring them myself. That day, I bent across the most elegant and piercing cross of my life. My teammate, Landon Donovan, headed it past the Mexican keeper to seal the victory. To date, it is one of the most remembered goals in U.S. soccer history.

In my quest to win for the glory of my nation, I also enjoyed personal triumph. I take this life lesson to bed with me each night. I am now retired. I have a beautiful wife and three amazing children. I know that when I act for the greater good of my family and my community, personal reward will naturally follow.

As an ambassador, I look to instill this World Cup lesson in those around me. I encourage players to try their best in their games for both themselves and their teammates. I cringe when parents pay their kids for goals or home runs. The intrinsic joy of sport is extremely powerful and far-reaching. Self-pride and fulfillment are priceless.

Finding the best in yourself for the success of a team also breeds brilliant camaraderie. This is exemplified beautifully on the fields of my middle son, who has special needs. His special-needs team has a way of brewing up a unique brand of team chemistry. This intangible aura also has a way of rubbing off on the non-disabled team that lines up against them. All the players, abled or disabled, compete in the utmost spirit of sportsmanship and pure love of athletics. Whether they wheel off or run off, all emerge victorious within.

Ultimately, whether it be on a youth recreational field or a World Cup stage, positive team unity plays an illusive role in success. You cannot buy, build, or bottle team synergy. It is something that comes from inside the souls of the players who take the field.

In Jeonju, on June 17, 2002, we stepped onto the field as a unified front. Patriotism was our twelfth man. I am proud to be an American, and I am proud to be a member of the most successful United States Men's National Team in World Cup history.

Intimidating the Champions

by Emile M'Bouh M'Bouh

I was training in Portugal when I received it—the message I had been waiting for all my life. It was the message that confirmed I had made the Cameroon squad for the 1990 World Cup in Italy. This is what every football player across the globe dreams of, the pinnacle of any career—representing my country on the world's biggest stage.

We had qualified for only our second ever World Cup by winning our group, which contained ourselves, Nigeria, Gabon, and Angola, before overcoming Tunisia in a two-legged play-off.

To prepare for the World Cup, we travelled to Yugoslavia, where we spent an entire month. We worked so hard. I remember that at this training camp, we decided we would just go to the World Cup and have fun—use the opportunity to show the world who Cameroonians truly were.

We had been drawn in a group with Romania, the Soviet Union, and the current world champions—Argentina, with the one and only Diego Maradona. He was the best player in the world at the time, widely respected and admired in Africa. But we didn't care. I said to myself, "He is just another football player."

We played Argentina in our first game, and we went into it with everybody saying that we were going to get humiliated. They were almost making fun of us. Our pride was hurt, really hurt. We were determined to prove people wrong and show them just how hard Les Lions Indomptables could really play.

When we first went out onto the field to have a look around, travelling Cameroonians were already in the stadium, singing, dancing, and shouting. This was an extremely proud moment for us, and we all said, "This is our day. This is our time!"

When we returned to the changing room to prepare, we were taken to a large indoor field where we would warm up away from the crowds. I just wanted to be outside in the amazing atmosphere. We were meant to use half a field each, us and the Argentines, but we were the only team in there so we took the entire thing. Our warm-ups always incorporate singing, shouting, and dancing very loudly. This got us in the right frame of mind. When the Argentines finally arrived at the indoor facility, they did not want to come in. They were scared of us; we were intimidating the world champions with our passion. It was a very tense moment, but we did not care. We were there to show the world we had finally arrived.

Singing the national anthem was a very special moment for me. When you stand there with ten of your teammates, wearing your nation's colors, you realize that this is about more than just you, about more than just Cameroon. It is about Africa, and all our African friends, brothers, sisters, mothers, and fathers. I could feel the adrenaline pumping through my body.

I clearly remember the first minute of the game. The Argentine central midfielder had given the ball to Maradona, and I found myself the closest player to him. I wanted to set the tone for the game from the start, so I went in with an extremely hard tackle. As I threw myself in with all my might, I could feel Maradona's entire body. He was all muscle. I remember laughing with one of my teammates. "This guy is so strong. We are going to have a tough time here!" But we were just going to go for it and give it everything we had.

I received my first booking of the tournament in the second half for not retreating when setting up a wall to protect our goal from an

Argentina free kick in a dangerous position. This card would prove to have a bigger impact for me later on in the tournament.

I was not the only one on our team to go into the book. André Kana-Biyik was shown a straight red card, and in the last minute Benjamin Massing was given his marching orders for a second booking. Both times we lost a player, we did not let it daunt us. We believed that we could play one, two, three players down and still win. We told each other, "We don't change what we have started; we just go for it." If anything, the dismissals motivated us even more!

When the final whistle blew, confirming that we had just beaten the world champions and the world's best player, it was as though lightning had come over us. We were so happy. We felt as though we could go straight back out there and play another game. We were that high.

We all returned to the changing room and prayed. We thanked God as a team and as a nation. Then the singing started. We sang, sang, sang. When we returned to the hotel, our supporters had crowded outside. We joined them with the singing and the dancing. It was as though we had just won the World Cup itself. This result had shown us, as well as the rest of the world, that Cameroon was not scared of anybody. We could play anybody in the world without fear and with the passion of the African continent.

We beat Romania in our second group game before losing to the Soviet Union. This meant that we topped our group. In the second round, we faced Colombia, and this is where my yellow card in the Argentina game became significant as I was again booked, this time for a two-footed challenge. As this was my second booking of the tournament, I would miss the quarter-finals should we make it.

At the time, it had not hit home that I would miss out on the next game. It was only at half-time when the other players told me that I realized it. I thought to myself, "No problem, I am just going to keep playing."

We beat Colombia thanks to two goals from Roger Milla, who was turning out to be one of the best players of the whole competition. In the quarter-finals, we played England, minus myself, and with twenty-five minutes to go, Eugène Ekéké put us 2–1 up. We eventually lost the game 3–2 after extra time.

The World Cup is the only place where you can watch all the best teams in the world. It is special when you watch it on television, but when you are there, it is almost unbelievable. I remember saying to myself, "Gosh, I am here. I am the lucky one. I am going to make the most of this." When we travelled to Italy, Cameroon was suffering some severe political unrest. Our performance helped our people forget about this for a while, and we were happy to give people that piece of joy—only the World Cup can offer this relief.

The Awakening of a Nation

by Peter Mellor

was eighteen years old when England won the World Cup at
Wembley Stadium in 1966. Watching the late, great Sir Bobby
Moore lift that Jules Rimet Trophy filled me with immense pride
and emotion. Fifteen-plus years later, I was fortunate to be playing
with Sir Bobby, again at Wembley, and again in a final, this time the
Football Association Challenge Cup (FA Cup) final. Unfortunately,
Sir Bobby did not lift a trophy that day.

Fast-forward six years to 1981, and I moved to the United States.
I went on to play for the Edmonton Drillers in the North American
Soccer League (NASL). Over here in the States, it was all about baseball,
(American) football, basketball, and then ice hockey. Miles down the
pecking order eventually came the sport I loved: soccer.

The USA qualified for their first World Cup in forty years in 1990
and went to the tournament in Italy with little more than a team of
college kids. There was no professional league in the country at that
stage, and the NASL had all but collapsed, so even qualifying was a great
achievement in itself. In their second game, they fell to a very narrow
1–0 defeat to the mighty Italians. I feel that this game pinpointed the
moment that U.S. soccer started the revolution.

In 1991, the then U.S. Head Coach, Bob Gansler, asked me to
oversee the goalkeeper program at all levels below the men's full team

for the United States Soccer Federation (USSF). This was all still before there was a professional league in the country. From 1991 to 2003, I was very proud to have been the national goalkeeper coach for some very talented U.S. youth sides, and I saw first-hand how they were starting to develop into players who could compete on the world stage for the very first time in the nation's soccer history.

I remember the 1994 World Cup on these shores well. I attended all the games with the U17 squad. Every time I went to the stadium for a game, it seemed completely full. It was an amazing sight, seeing my adopted country finally showing a love for my sport and in such a passionate way. Having so much world-class soccer on their—or should I say *our*—doorsteps really exposed the U.S. public to the game on a nationwide level for the first time—and we adored it!

I also remember being at the magnificent Rose Bowl in Los Angeles for the USA v. Colombia game. Neither of the teams had won their first group game (we had drawn with Switzerland, and the Colombians had lost, if memory serves me right), so the pressure was extremely high for both sides to win since a defeat would all but eliminate the loser from the competition. It just was not in the script for the hosts—a nation that was only just finding its feet in the soccer world and rapidly growing to love it—to go out in the group stages. All the hype surrounding the sport at that moment would surely, just as quickly as it had appeared, die back down, and soccer would return to its low position on the pecking order of U.S. sports.

Thankfully, we managed to come away with a 2–1 victory, which proved to be enough to qualify us for the next round. Sadly, the gloss was taken off this victory a few days later as the Colombian center back, Andrés Escobar, who scored an own goal to put the U.S. one up in that game, was shot and killed upon his return to his country, supposedly because of that goal.

We—and I now refer to the USA team as "we" since my entire family has such a strong emotional attachment to U.S. soccer—well, we eventually got knocked out in the round of 16 to eventual winners Brazil, also by only one goal. This was a massive achievement. I could see how this tournament had changed an entire nation, and it was a great time to be a part of soccer in this country. The hype and enthusiasm generated by the '94 World Cup were picked up by Major League Soccer (MLS), and they simply rode that wave. I would say that they are still riding it! It truly was the awakening of a nation.

In the '90s, the kids that I worked with in the U.S. youth teams were, in my opinion, as technically good as anybody. Some really talented boys were coming through. However, they were not tactically aware enough. They were just not at the right level. They didn't know how to perform on the big stage; they were deer caught in the headlights, overwhelmed.

That story is starting to change. We now have players who play all over the world and compete for the highest honors. The U.S. Men's National Team, on its day, can beat anybody, and I mean anybody, in the world. Throughout my years as a coach in this country, I have worked with some really talented kids, such as Tim Howard, Clint Dempsey, Landon Donovan, and Kyle Beckerman, to name just a few. These guys have gone on to make up the greatest U.S. national team of all time, and the expectations for them in 2014 are higher than ever. It makes me emotional and proud at the same time to watch these players I had as young, raw kids holding their own on the world stage and in a competition I have so many fond memories of from my younger years. I feel as though I was there at the start and saw the beginnings of this revolution. The U.S. team now epitomizes the passion and patriotism of the World Cup. How much further can U.S. soccer evolve? Well, I guess we will just have to wait for Brazil in the summer to see!

Goodfella to Goalkeeper

by Shep Messing

I grew up in the Bronx. Like any kid growing up there, I played stickball and baseball. My heroes were Mickey Mantle and Jackie Robinson. I didn't touch a soccer ball until I was sixteen, but here I was four years later in the Olympic stadium in Munich, playing for U.S. National Team. It was the 1972 Olympics, and it was as close as I was going to get to the 1974 World Cup finals to be held in the same stadium two years later. I was the starting goalkeeper in what was fondly remembered in red, white and blue soccer history as the "wilderness years"—we never got close to qualifying!

Although I never had the privilege of playing in the World Cup finals, I have been lucky enough to play with or against eight of the top ten on the list of all-time best players who have graced the world's greatest stage: Pelé, Zico, Carlos Alberto, Beckenbauer, Eusébio, Johan Cruyff, Gerd Müller, and Diego Maradona. In addition, I have been blessed to have been able to commentate live on World Cup matches in the USA 1994, Japan and Korea 2002, Germany 2006, and South Africa in 2010. For this year's World Cup, I will be in Brazil working for ESPN again.

The World Cup finals is an experience like no other. Each one surpasses the last. Each time, it gets bigger, better, and more memorable. It is the meeting of the world's greatest national teams and highest profile superstars doing battle over four weeks to find out who truly is the best.

In 1994, the United States hosted the finals. Those three weeks will live long in my memory as a truly amazing experience. Watching the World Cup reach the consciousness of the American public was an unbelievable feeling. At the stadiums, the tournament broke all attendance records; World Cup fever had infected the U.S. The bars and streets were packed. In New York, Chicago, Los Angeles and all over the nation, supporters were wearing the colors and waving flags. Three hundred million people were ready to absorb and embrace the World Cup finals as the greatest sporting event ever.

I remember going to dinner in New York with Pelé after the Ireland v. Italy game at Giants Stadium. He had tears in his eyes because of the positive impact soccer was having in the U.S. It was the fulfillment of a dream that started way back in the North American Soccer League with the New York Cosmos in 1976/77, when he first came over to play. He had hoped and hoped for this, and now it was a reality. When I speak to Pelé and Beckenbauer and other legends of the world game, they don't talk about a specific moment of the World Cup. Although many have won it and you would think that this would be their over-riding memory, it is not. They are proud of what they achieved, and there is a "look" that all the greats have. They love the legacy aspect of their achievements; it's worn like a silk handkerchief in their pocket. There is an inner peace and knowledge that their greatest moments and memories are the foundations that help support the wall of new World Cup experiences and achievements.

My first World Cup final was not as a broadcaster, but as a spectator. The year was 1998, and the World Cup was in France. The tournament was a masterpiece of attacking flair, and everyone dreamed of a France v. Brazil final. This dream became a reality, and the final was a match-up of the current champions, Brazil, and the hosts, France. Paris was at fever pitch, an outpouring of emotion and expectation. France had never won a World Cup, and the feeling was that this was their time. I was a guest of the Nigerian coach, Bora Milutinović, and our party met for breakfast at 10:00 AM. By then, the party across the nation was in full swing. The streets were packed, and everything was red, white and blue. The journey to the stadium should have been a short car ride, but no traffic was moving, so we soaked up the atmosphere and walked through the street to the magnificent Stade de France. We arrived two hours before the game, and already the stands were full. Cries of "allez les blèus" were ringing around the stadium. The game did not disappoint. It was played in true World Cup spirit, end to end attacking—a real celebration of how the game should be played. France was the eventual winner, 3–0, and it marked the beginning of a party to end all parties. It went on for days—I think we got back to the hotel two days later. The true spirit of the World Cup was displayed. The disappointed Brazilian fans were gracious in defeat, and by 2:00 AM they were dancing with everyone, too.

The World Cup is always magical. Every experience is different, but the spirit and message are always the same. My World Cup greatest moment is waiting for the next one, the sense of anticipation and the endless possibilities, the highs and lows, the heartache, jubilation, heroic wins, the David versus Goliath moments, and the triumph of the human spirit to persevere.

Special Moment
in a Pizzeria

by Rachel Nuzzolese

When that gold medal was placed around my neck, a feeling came over me. I thought back to when I was sitting at the local Italian pizzeria with my family back in 2006. The World Cup final, Italy v. France, was playing on a big, flat-screen TV. I was surrounded by Italian flags, Italian jerseys, and the best pizza in town. The restaurant was packed with anxious Italians all waiting for a goal. I remember how nervous I was when the game went down to a penalty shoot-out. I knew exactly what they were feeling, but I couldn't imagine being in front of a crowd that big. It was all coming down to one kick. The ref blew the whistle, and everyone in the restaurant got silent. Fabio Grosso hit home the winning penalty to have Italy win the World Cup for the first time in my lifetime. Champagne was flying all over the place, and everyone in the restaurant was hugging one another, chanting, "Italia! Italia! Italia!" I knew from that moment that that's what I wanted to do. Just watching the win, I realized how important this was for the players, coaches, fans and, most importantly, the country. It really hit me that soccer could bring many people together. Soccer had always been a major part of my life, but that very special moment in a pizzeria was when I decided it had to be my life.

It all started at the age of three. Dad would always say before every game and practice, "Rachel, don't stop until the ball is in the…" I would jump up and scream, "NET!" My mindset every game was to never stop working hard and make sure I scored. This goal-scoring mindset continued throughout my career. There is a one-of-a-kind feeling about scoring that I can't explain. It is an enormous rush of happiness that takes over your body. It reminded me of all the hard work and dedication I put into this game. I knew that all my soccer training, strength training, sacrifices, and playing on numerous club teams were helping me develop as a person and a player.

I worked hard to improve my game, make better decisions on the field, and be the best teammate I could be. During my freshman year in high school, I was named All-State and All-American. But nothing prepared me for this moment. It finally hit me when I was walking out of the tunnel in my United States Women's National Team jersey. I put my hand across my heart and started bawling my eyes out when I heard the National Anthem play. It was such an emotional experience. I was representing my country at the U17 Women's World Cup qualifiers in Trinidad and Tobago. This was my first career start for my country against El Salvador, and I was super nervous. I went on to score a hat trick and played one of the best games of my life. After the game, I was told by one of the soccer ambassadors that I was the first American woman to score three goals in the U17 Women's World Cup qualifying game. We went on to win the qualifying bracket, and I received that gold medal.

All of these experiences have shaped me into the person I am today. From watching Italy win that World Cup, I knew that I wanted to do the same for the women's USA team. It still gives me chills every four years when I watch the men's World Cup. My memories of being able to play for my country after all of the work and commitment that I dedicated to the sport will stay with me forever. Nowadays, when I train young men and women, I can see in their eyes the excitement and feeling of happiness that I got when I was younger. Every time I watch the men's World Cup, I can see it on their faces, as well. Nothing gets me more excited than seeing the passion and commitment from those proud players and coaches representing their country. Not many people get to have their entire nation supporting them and bursting with pride at their success. The World Cup is the pinnacle of that, and it is this event, every four years, that I have to thank for reaching the heights that I did.

More than Just a Football Competition

by John Pantsil

It was an emotional feeling to see the African continent join hands together to support us, the Ghanaian team, the Black Stars of Ghana. I realised that I was not playing only for my motherland, but for the whole African continent. I saw Kenyans supporting us; I saw Malayans supporting us; I saw Togolese supporting us; I saw Ethiopians supporting us. I saw the mighty South Africans supporting us and calling Ghana *Bafana Bafana* (a nickname given to the national side by its fans; in Zulu, it translates literally as "the boys, the boys"). And many more African countries gave us massive support and trust; an enormous swell of passion and determination swept in from an entire continent. Two days before the game, I was watching the sports news about the chance of Ghana becoming the first African nation to ever make the World Cup semi-finals. All we had to do was beat Uruguay, and Luis Suárez, in that week's quarter-final!

On the day of the match, I woke up around 6:00 AM to pray. Forty-five minutes later, I heard the vuvuzela, with music and people singing, "Bafana Bafana"! I quickly opened my window to see. I felt like I was already on the field. The road to the stadium was packed full of African flags! Fans were shouting, "Ghana! Bafana Bafana," while vuvuzela music and drumming echoed all around.

At warm-ups on the field, Europeans, Americans, Brazilians, and

Asians were also supporting us, their national flags mixing with our continent's flags. When they played our National Anthem, I felt the ground shaking, as if it was telling my teammates and me that we were holding millions of people's hearts—especially those of our African men, women, grandpas, grandmums, and youth—in our hands until the end of the game. It was an emotional feeling and a wake-up call to me.

During kick-off, my mind settled down to work as a team player—taking on my responsibilities on the field of play, making sure my position was well defended before attacking, keeping my discipline and concentration based on how the game was going. Yet I was hearing only one sound—the vuvuzela! We scored the first goal, but they came back, and ninety minutes finished in a 1–1 draw. So off we went to extra time. We won a free kick that was close to their goal area. I picked up the ball and spoke to it, "God help us. This free kick should give us a goal."

After speaking to the ball, I placed it on the ground and kicked it into their penalty box. It was a 50/50 chance for us to score. We won a strong header through Dominic Adiyiah towards the goal. We all thought it was in, and some of us started to celebrate! Then the ball was saved by the hands of Suárez, the South American forward. A penalty was given to us. We were happy when it was nearly time for the game to finish. This would be the final kick of the game, and it could put us in the semi-finals—for Africa!

We missed the penalty. It was a shock to my teammates and me. We continued to push until we reached a penalty shoot-out. We lost it on penalties, and I can barely express how bad we felt. Tears, heartbreak, crying. Some of us couldn't even eat or drink water. It felt as if a lot of people "lost their lives" that day, both in Ghana and other African countries. I'm still in tears just thinking about it!

I enjoyed every second and minute of the 2010 FIFA World Cup in South Africa. I got to meet different people, different players from all over the world, coming together in friendship despite different languages and personalities. I saw red and yellow cards being shown to top players, top players missing easy goals, top players missing penalties, top referees making mistakes. The World Cup brought us all together to become one nation and one people. Every World Cup is a special occasion for footballers. It makes them feel special and important to their nation. It also gives players more exposure to different clubs, which polishes their game standard.

The people of Ghana couldn't wait to see us back home after our great performance. A big convoy accompanied us through the capital city, Accra, with drumming, music and dancing. The following day, we were invited by Ghanaian President John Evans Atta Mills to his castle. He congratulated us for our performance, saying, "Well done, my children, I am proud of you. May God bless you for putting the country of Ghana on the world map." Our names were all over Africa. We received so much respect from our people in Ghana; families were happy and proud of us. A lot of companies in Ghana donated money, food and drinks to the Football Association in appreciation. Students were actually excited about going to classes. The police treated us like we were special (but only if we behaved!). Banks gave us special treatment. Kids on the streets ran up to us to shake our hands. The 2010 World Cup was more to Ghana than just a football competition. It unified our entire country and made me proud to be Ghanaian.

Larry Mullen
Saved the Day!

by Mark Patterson

T he die was cast the moment the draw was made. Republic of Ireland (ROI) was to face a rematch of their painful exit from Italia '90, the defeat that deflated our entire nation. We were drawn to face Italy in our opening game of USA '94, and I was there.

I was also skint (poor) but skilful enough to conspire with close friends in the States, who purported to cover my costs in return for face-value match tickets, which in fairness were like hens' teeth. Happily, I had tickets in abundance — three for each qualifying game, courtesy of professional ties with the glorious League of Ireland club, Drogheda United, to whom I am forever grateful!

How could my loving wife object to free travel and considering the match tickets were contingent on me travelling? Still, I hinted and hesitated for months until finally, just one week prior to departure, I announced I was definitely going. "Don't come back!" was her response. Hell hath no fury, for sure.

So the reunion began under threat of my divorce. A decade after we'd left school, five of us gathered in Boston — me, Baz, Gillo, Dylan, and our host AG, one of Boston's finest — all of whose names are unchanged to expose the guilty!

After several days of solid drinking and enjoying preliminary games in numerous Boston bars, we set off for New Jersey in a rented

Lincoln Town Car. It was dawn on the day of the game, and we were two tickets short. Thankfully, the Drogheda connection came through again, and we headed directly to the team hotel to make good on this shortfall before breakfast!

As we chowed down on what would be our only meal of the day, we slowly began to realise we were surrounded by those we'd come to idolise: Tommy Coyne, Big Jack (Charlton — the Head Coach), Andy Townsend, Kevin Sheedy, Packie Bonner, all dotted around the restaurant. Before long, the entire ROI squad appeared, and Jack led the players on a leisurely stroll around the grounds.

Giddy as kids at Christmas, we retired to the bar the instant it opened and downed our first of many that day. The place was soon buzzing, as were we! Dear beer flowed freely. To our amazement, senior players mingled easily and posed for photographs with anyone who asked. Terry Phelan, Packie Bonner, Ray Houghton and Paul McGrath all lined up with us, while a queue of happy photo hunters formed behind us.

Becoming frenzied, we began grabbing anyone we remotely recognised and squeezed into the frame with them. This included someone with a remarkable resemblance to the Irish assistant manager, Maurice Setters (who it wasn't) and old-timer, Mark Lawrenson (ex-ROI and Liverpool). Gentlemen all.

Niall Quinn, injured and reporting for RTÉ, told us that the three amigos — twenty-one-year-old Gary Kelly, Jason McAteer and Phil Babb — weren't allowed down from the team floor for fear they might lose the run of themselves before the game, just like we were doing! Roy Keane? Not really his scene we concluded, but we did catch a glimpse of his steely stare as he boarded the bus a little later. There might even have been a slight hint of a smile; we are not sure.

Ultimate Irish hero, Paul McGrath, was especially generous with his time, despite the fact that his wife and kids had just arrived at the precise moment we mobbed him. We owe Paul an apology still!

Amidst the commotion, as we cheered the boys onto the bus, it dawned on us almost too late that we were likely to miss kick-off by the time we reached the stadium and got to our seats — especially

51

Baz, Gillo and Dylan, whose seats were up in the gods. They probably should have brought binoculars!

No fear, with Boston Police badge in hand! One quick look was all it took for New Jersey State Police to slot us in behind the team bus and escort us all the way, along with the official convoy, sirens wailing, helicopters overhead, U2 blaring on the stereo, making mayhem much to the amusement of passersby and those on the bus in front! God bless America!

Then the real fun began. Giants Stadium was a steaming cauldron, decked out top to bottom in green, white and gold, seething with raucous Irish all roaring for the Boys in Green and scarcely an Italian to be seen.

I kept the best seats in the house for AG and me. Six rows back from the halfway line, right behind the dugout, we sat directly behind none other than Larry Mullen from U2 (and I may owe him an apology, too)! What a beautiful day, and it was about to get better.

This vantage point gave us the perfect view of Houghton's mesmerizing lofted shot on 12 minutes, as it floated for an eternity, sailing gracefully in a high arc over helpless, retreating Pagliuca, before bulging softly in the back of the net, almost dreamlike!

Pandemonium! Absolute ecstasy! Jumping, screaming, roaring, kissing, hugging, cheering, crying, laughing, choking, shouting, high-fiving, diving, surging, falling, and eventually sagging back into our seats, smiling insanely, soaked in beer and sweat. Steeped in pure joy!

Then we melted. Not the team, but AG, me and 80,000 other Irish lads, freckles or no. Boiling in 110-degree heat, the oppressive humidity and zealous celebrations stole our breath. We watched with mounting anxiety as the Boys in Green held their own in gruelling conditions. They did not wilt! They matched Italy toe to toe, but ultimately we prayed for the whistle to blow. When it did, we surged forward, screaming wildly at the bench, where they were also ecstatic. Mick Byrne, kit man, tossed water bottles to the crowd, possibly saving us from death by dehydration.

The return journey to Boston was abysmal. Severely hoarse and utterly exhausted, we drove directly back in a six-hour journey into endless night, bitterly disappointed to bypass Manhattan at the designated driver's behest. Adrenaline ebbed away, replaced by a pounding hangover. Right then, I wished I was home, where the nation's celebrations would rage into the night. Two days later, deep in trepidation, I headed home alone to Ireland.

Fortunately for me, we'd been caught on TV! Our pre-match exuberance outside the team hotel was beamed back home live, where my wonderful wife was watching on a large screen. It was a clear-cut case of "so near and yet so far." All was instantly forgiven!

Just like the team, I returned to a hero's welcome! My only trophy was a signed jersey that also reads:

"To Clodagh (my wife), with love, Larry"

We remain happily married to this day, thanks to Larry!

The World's Game

by Christopher Sullivan

All my life, football has blessed me. One of my most memorable recollections of the game was when I was eleven years old. My grandmother took me to Italy, where I first heard the sounds that would sing in my heart the rest of my life — the sounds of the ball on cobblestone streets echoing across the city. I have strong memories of the ball at my feet and the way it felt. In my encounters with other kids, our shared passion for the ball became our common language and the source of our mutual respect. I could never quite call them strangers again.

With my father and my best friend, I travelled to Mexico City in 1986 to witness live my first World Cup. It was Argentina and West Germany in the final, along with 120,000 other delirious fans at Estadio Azteca. The atmosphere was electric, absolutely unbelievable, and nothing could compare until my opportunity to play for the U.S. National Team.

Like the song from my childhood, I found myself again on the cobblestone streets of Italy, which still reverberated as I strode into Stadio Olimpico with my World Cup teammates to play against the host country and tournament favorite, Italia. Standing next to my friend and teammate, John Harkes, any attempt we made to talk or even yell to each other was drowned out by the roar of the host supporters. We couldn't hear; all we could do was grin and shake our heads. The game was tight, and the din of Italian fans chanting "Forza Azzurri" was deafening. As the game progressed, Italy clung to a goal lead, but we played with heart and determination. At one point, we strung together twenty-three passes as the whistles of disappointment rang down upon our opponent. In the end, we had gained the respect of the Italian players and fans. When the final whistle blew, we received an ovation from the hosts. Football is truly a beautiful game.

That was 1990. In 2006, the World Cup was in Germany. I was there as an analyst covering the France v. Italy final at the Olympic Stadium in Berlin where, in the 1936 Olympics, Jesse Owens made Olympic history with his medal success. I had been fortunate to play in that same city as a professional when I was with Hertha Berlin. It was an amazing feeling after thirteen years to return to the stadium and witness the World Cup final with legendary Colombian Carlos "El Pibe" Valderrama.

Now it's off to Rio de Janeiro for the 2014 World Cup in Brazil as a TV analyst. My magical journey continues, but I will always remember the beginning—the cobblestone streets, the sound and the feel of the ball on my feet, and the laughter of children playing the world's game.

My Mexican Family

by Kim Tate

My first World Cup experience was in 2010, when I watched Landon Donovan score the game winner against Algeria. It was a brilliant moment in time for U.S. soccer fans, and I cried tears of joy with many of them.

Growing up a USA fan, I loved soccer. I made my way onto the pitch once in a while, but for me, watching the game from different teams around the globe, especially Latin America, gave me the biggest thrill.

I come from a family of very limited means. I grew up in a single-parent home. My mother often had to work three jobs to place food on the table, put me through school, and give us a life when my father passed away. I was four when he died. Mom never remarried nor had other children. Our relationship, at times, was tumultuous.

During middle school and high school, I had a best friend, Veronica, who is Mexican. Her family took me in when I could no longer live with my mother, and they treated me like their own. Their love and acceptance of me came during a time when I was the most vulnerable and impressionable. I went to their parties, they took me shopping, and I accompanied them to bigger family gatherings and events. I would occasionally go back to my mom's house when I missed her, but I felt that my real home and sense of belonging were with Veronica and her family — "my Mexican family," as they became affectionately known.

I've always had a fondness for other cultures, especially for the

Mexican culture. My Mexican family was a blessing when I needed them, and they've continued to be a blessing in my current professional life. Not a day goes by when I don't think about them and apply the values they instilled in me to my own circumstances. They enabled me to step out of my comfort zone, approach another culture — although I was sometimes met with resistance — and write about their sport to educate and entertain fans on a global level. And I've just barely scratched the surface.

It took a lot of jobs, confusion, and moving around for me to realize how much I truly loved writing about the sport in Mexico. When I go to games in Tijuana, I get looks. When I show up in Mexican restaurants to see if they'll play a series of Liga MX games on three different channels, I get looks. It's considered rare (and odd) for an all-American-looking, blonde-haired, blue-eyed female to be so immersed in something like Mexican soccer. I go through periods of insecurity and fear because I'm a female covering a sport in a country where I've never lived, worried that people will be skeptical of me.

Most of the time, though, it's quite the opposite. I've made more friends covering the Mexican leagues ahead of the World Cup than I can count. In only ten months covering Mexico — from L.A. to Tijuana, Guadalajara to Mexico City — soccer has shaped my life. I've embraced new friendships. I've been able to give and receive blessings. I've fallen in love and experienced the pains of heartbreak. I've had the opportunity to do charity work and experience life in another country when I make the trek to Mexico to cover games. On a professional front, I've received freelance offers from U.K.-based publications, and have been on the radio and TV. I'm building something — all because of one sport leading up to one competition.

As I move forward, the biggest goal at the forefront of my mind is to use soccer as a platform to expose the beauty of the Mexican culture. I want to get to know the people behind the games — their stories, struggles, and triumphs — and pass those on to my friends in the United States and beyond.

My mom passed away on July 13, 2010. I was twenty-six. While we were never close, we developed a unique relationship in the months leading up to her sudden passing. Coincidentally, I had reunited with my Mexican family after four years on the very day I received the call with the news. While I was mourning my loss at their home, I found an email my mom had sent to me about a week before she departed. It was casual and sweet, just as you'd expect a "check-in email" from a mom to read. It was her last form of communication with me. I don't know if she sensed that it was her time, but she left me a paragraph of life advice pertaining to my career, telling me to take risks when they seem scary, put myself out there, and embrace being in the public eye and interacting with other people and cultures. At the time, she and I had no idea I'd wind up so immersed in another culture woven in with soccer as an intended career path.

The final game of the World Cup is scheduled for July 13, 2014, four years to the day of her passing. I like to think in this four-year window that her advice, the path life carved out for me, and my passion for the sport have come full circle. I can only hope that my continued hard work will pay off and allow me to explore more of Mexico, cover our sport, and share the stories of its people for the greater good.

Scots in the Shadows as Old Foe Brazil Prepares to Samba

by Ian Thomson

Scotland's soccer team strode into the Stade de France in June 1998 with the eyes of the world upon them, while out marched the sizzling world champions from Brazil. Ronaldo, Rivaldo, Bebeto, Dunga, and Roberto Carlos were among the yellow-shirted superstars linking arms as they prepared to defend their FIFA World Cup crown.

The Seleção took four minutes to score the tournament's opening goal and drain the skittish excitement from the Triple Kirks Pub in Aberdeen where I, and about 200 others, had sprinted to after finishing work that afternoon.

Some friends had traveled to Paris with Scotland's official 5,000-strong fan allocation. They later bragged of triumphing in five-a-side battles between kilted Scots and canny Brazilians in the shadow of the Eiffel Tower. My adventure was being hemmed into claustrophobic surroundings with a crowd that still believed our team could overcome its apparent inferiority complex.

We received a penalty kick shortly before half-time. John Collins coolly slotted his shot wide of Taffarel's dive, prompting a euphoric eruption and torrents of beer raining down from hoisted glasses. Hope had been restored. False hope. We should have known.

Brazil's marauding full-back, Cafu, burst into our penalty area late in the game, forcing veteran goalkeeper, Jim Leighton, to block his close-range effort. The ball rebounded against helpless defender, Tommy Boyd, and trickled into Leighton's net. An eerie silence shrouded the room—the sound of gravity.

The Scottish World Cup experience is characterized by daring-ness to dream and the crushing reality of defeat. We have reached the tournament eight times, and we have yet to escape the opening group phase. Blind optimism precedes each attempt. The law of averages will favor us eventually. Yet every journey unfolds like that of a wandering nomad traversing the desert who discovers that the shimmering oasis on the horizon is a figment of his imagination.

Scotland's 1982 campaign is the first that I recall watching on TV. Gordon Strachan, one of my earliest heroes from Alex Ferguson's dominant Aberdeen team, created three goals in a 5–2 rout of New Zealand that cranked up the feeling that this was our turn.

A 4–1 thumping from the free-flowing Brazil of Zico, Éder, Falcão and Sócrates left us needing to beat the Soviet Union to progress. My father remained notably impassive when Alan Hansen crashed into defensive partner Willie Miller, freeing an opponent who duly put the Russians ahead in the closing minutes. He knew the eventual misery of being a Scotland fan.

The flame-haired Strachan raised our hopes again four years later when he darted across West Germany's penalty box in the Mexican sunshine to lash a shot beyond goalkeeper Harald Schumacher. It was 1–0 to the Scots. Strachan sprinted behind the goal to celebrate with jubilant fans before finding that his 5-foot-6-inch frame could not hurdle the advertising boards surrounding the field. Strachan's shortcomings mirrored those of our national team. Minor glories filled us with the misplaced confidence that we could thrive among the big boys. Strachan's embarrassment as he hopped in vain, trying to lift his leg over the hoardings, resonated with all of us. Deep within, we knew we would look sheepish when forced to abandon our lofty thoughts.

Last-game heroics, and Scotland's inability to produce them, are woven into our World Cup story. It was a lesson I began to understand as West Germany fought back to compound our opening loss to Denmark. Even ten-year-old kids develop a sinking feeling when reality sets in.

Victory over Uruguay would still have sneaked Scotland into the second round. A first-minute red card issued to José Batista for a despicable lunge at Strachan brought that shimmering oasis back into view. Uruguay's ten men hacked their way to a depressing stalemate, leaving the image of Steve Nicol's timid side-footer that was cleared from the goal line etched in the collective psyche of the Tartan Army.

The 1990 World Cup arrived as I reached the perfect age, my early teens, for it to consume every moment. I had suitably matured enough to appreciate and devour what was happening on the field, yet free from the commitments that later encroach upon a month of soccer viewing. And I was still young enough to sport Scotland's natty replica jersey without it being considered a faux pas by my increasingly fashion-conscious peers.

Somebody else had little problem with wearing soccer merchandise, which I discovered upon returning to the changing rooms at Aberdeen's Hazlehead Park after playing in a youth league game. My shirt had been swiped from its peg. My disappointment was a harbinger of what was to follow.

Costa Rica, written off as no-hopers by Scotland's blinkered media, acted as the traditional opening-game spoiler. A win over Sweden left us needing to tie Brazil to reach the second round. Scotland kept Careca and Romário quiet on this occasion, but Jim Leighton's fumble from Alemão's shot allowed substitute Müller to give the South Americans a late lead.

Our suffering was not quite over. A desperate stoppage-time attack saw a loose ball dropping to Maurice Johnston on Brazil's 6-yard line. My father and I rose from the sofa in anticipation of our center-forward sweeping the ball into either corner of Taffarel's net. Johnston's connection fizzed straight at the sprawling goalkeeper, deflecting off Taffarel's torso before clearing Brazil's crossbar. Typical Scotland. Despondency to delirium to the doldrums with a few thwacks of the ball.

Sixteen years have passed since our last World Cup appearance in France. The pain of our absence again this summer is at least mitigated by the avoidance of further anguish.

The Earthquake

by Nick Webster

I've experienced earthquakes before. Living in Southern California, they are a fact of life. They always catch you by surprise though, and can, depending on the Richter scale, set the heart and other parts of the body racing.

The city port of Busan, South Korea, is located along the Ring of Fire, an earthquake zone. On June 4, 2002, it experienced seismic activity that wasn't measured by any geological organization, however; the jolt was felt around the world.

Before the 2002 World Cup, jointly hosted by South Korea and Japan, South Korea was predominantly known by the Western world for the Korean conflict, good cars, and electronics. Football was not a blip on the radar, although their fighting cousins from the north had once ventured to the World Cup quarter-finals in 1966 before losing to Eusébio's Portugal 5–3, in one of the all-time classic matches.

Entering the tournament in 2002, South Korea, coached by the legendary Dutch rainmaker, Guus Hiddink, was considered to be more than a curiosity factor and a benevolent host. The experts deemed a first-round exit a distinct possibility.

The train I took from the capital, Seoul, to Busan on the morning of June fourth was full to capacity, but eerily silent. Each compartment was standing room only for the four-hour journey. It felt more like a funeral procession than the beginning of South Korea's World Cup.

I arrived at the Busan Asiad Main Stadium three hours before the kick-off to comment on the atmosphere and excitement of the South Korean fans, but it was as much of a bust as the train—nothing was happening around the stadium either.

In the pressroom, located in the bowels of the stadium, the journalistic crowd wandered around, waiting for something—anything—to happen.

At 6:15 PM local time, I felt the first tremor. It felt like a 2.3 on the Richter scale. That was followed moments later by another tremor and then another jolt.

Nervous but not overly concerned, I asked a fellow journalist, "Are we experiencing an earthquake?"

He replied, "No, the South Korean fans have arrived."

Now, I've been to stadiums that move. La Bombonera, the home of Argentina's Boca Juniors, comes to mind as the stands literally sway in unison to the faithful, but this was different. This was urgent, powerful, and thrilling. The concrete beneath my feet was sending shock waves throughout my body.

Fifteen minutes before kick-off, I made my way up to the press box through a combination of stairwells and elevators. I moved towards the media entrance and was hit by a concussion of sound. It wasn't a regular football sound, though. This was something different, but I couldn't place it.

Next to go was my vision. It appeared as if the entire stadium, except for the press hacks, was wearing red, and this heaving, swaying, gyrating mass was moving as one.

This wasn't your normal football crowd... this was the Red Devils.

I've seen many football crowds, but never experienced one so organized and passionate. Every fan I could see took up the chants. Neck muscles strained, eyes bulged, and voices soared—and we still hadn't heard the National Anthem as the two teams entered the field of play.

As the first notes of "Aegukga," the South Korean anthem, began, a huge Taegukgi, the national flag, was unfurled at the far end of the stadium, covering almost every supporter. It moved in time with the anthem while tears streamed down the faces of supporters close to me.

This was turning into a quasi-religious experience, but it wasn't until the ball was in play for the first time that the moment hit me.

The first throw-in won by the Koreans was greeted with almost maniacal hysteria.

It was obvious that this football team was playing for every single South Korean in a competition that was more about national pride than a game of football.

The first attack by the Poles brought shrieks that would shame a Hollywood horror movie. They were high-pitched, terrified and filled with an absurd amount of tension. We could feel the air crackle like in the moments before a storm. The first goal would be everything, and it had to be scored by South Korea or their World Cup would be over before it had even begun.

Poland hadn't read the script and kept on looking dangerous, especially in counter-attack situations. The screams of abject horror from the home fans as the Eastern Europeans advanced at pace made me think of the teenage girls who had lost their minds at the sight of the Beatles at Shea Stadium.

And then it happened: Hwang Sun-Hong in the 26th minute with a pure swing of his left boot.

Goals are received the world over with a roar, especially by the home fans, but this noise didn't come from the throat; it came from a place that South Koreans had never been before.

In a land where emotions are controlled, where customs and conventions are to be obeyed, football fans hadn't figured out where they belonged until now.

This roar was hundreds, if not thousands of years in the making, and it was felt not just in Busan, but also in every street throughout the peninsula because millions of souls were roaring as one.

On the field in Busan, the players rushed to Hiddink. He knew what it meant, and his players, who may have had doubts beforehand, were now filled with the most important cocktail in all of football... namely, belief.

Belief, when it comes, has a momentum all its own. The South Korean football team, the South Korean fans, and the entire country of South Korea had waited a long time for this moment to come. But now that it had arrived, they drank from the bottle of belief like it was the last bottle they'd ever see, touch, taste, hear, or feel.

History tells us that Guus Hiddink and his team achieved what no other Asian team has ever done—they went on a roller-coaster ride to the semi-finals through luck, outrageous decisions, great skill, unbelievable teamwork and a massive dose of belief.

I was there the day they popped open that bottle, and it was—and has remained to this day—the most powerful experience I've ever felt at any sporting event, just like an earthquake.

Meet Our Contributors

Named to U.S. Soccer's All-Time Men's National Team Best XI, **Carlos Bocanegra** is a legendary figure in American soccer. Having debuted with the National Team in 2001, he went on to captain the team from 2007 until 2013. A two-time FIFA World Cup veteran (2006 and 2010), he has earned 110 caps and currently holds the record for most international goals scored by a U.S. defender with fourteen. Carlos has made more than 350 club appearances in a decorated career spanning across Europe and America. He is the current captain of MLS club side Chivas USA, and is the owner and founder of CB3 Sports Performance (cb3sportsperformance.com).

Andy Boyens moved from his native New Zealand to study at the University of New Mexico in 2004, where he was named a first-team All-American. Andy has played seventy games in the MLS for Toronto FC, Chivas USA, New York Red Bulls, and L.A. Galaxy. He has nineteen caps for the New Zealand national team and was part of the 2010 World Cup squad. He now coaches in his home country.

George Cohen MBE played right full back for England in the side that won the 1966 World Cup. He won 37 caps for England between 1964 and 1967. He is a Football Hall of Famer and was awarded the Most Excellent Order of the British Empire in 2000 for his role in England's 1966 success. He spent his entire club career playing for Fulham in England.

Tony Collins saw his first England game in 1964, and has travelled the world watching them ever since, including to destinations such as the USSR, East Germany, and Czechoslovakia. Tony is now retired and resides in the south of England with his wife, Fran. He has three daughters, a stepson and a stepdaughter. He also has four step-grandkids.

Niccolo Conte is a writer who watches and follows as much European football as he can, with a special interest in the Serie A and the Italian national team. While accumulating his thoughts and analysis on his blog, Soccer Wrap Up (www.soccerwrapup.blogspot.com), he writes for various other websites such as Soccerlens and World Soccer Talk.

Joe Frederik is from Amsterdam, the Netherlands, and is an avid football writer. He started WorldCupOfJoe.com in October 2012 to write about the 2014 FIFA World Cup in Brazil.

Asit Ganguli started India's first football magazine, *Cleat Beat*, in 2010. With a 100% paperless setup, it is a magazine designed for the future, catering to readers who are interested in the technical side of the game. The magazine is read in more than 185 countries. The *Cleat Beat* team has also set up a youth soccer network and run a coaching academy. Asit is also Managing Director at Blue Krill Brand Management in New Delhi.

Ben Jones is a radio sports announcer on 1116SEN in Melbourne, Australia, where he discusses soccer on a nightly basis. He follows the Melbourne Victory across the country, as well as the Australian national team, the Socceroos. He also works for CorcMedia Pty Ltd.

Matt Leaver is an avid football fan and has dedicated much of his life to following both the English national team and Fulham around England and Europe. Matt is a City & Guilds qualified plasterer and resides in Worthing in Southeast England with his wife, Loren, and son, Archie.

Eddie Lewis enjoyed a professional career that spanned sixteen years, playing extensively in both the United States and England. He tallied eighty-two caps, scoring ten goals for the U.S. National Team and represented his country at the 1999 Confederations Cup, 2002 FIFA World Cup, 2003 Confederations Cup, 2003 CONCACAF Gold Cup, and 2006 FIFA World Cup. Eddie is married and the proud father of three children. Since retiring in 2010, Eddie founded TOCA (tocafootball.com), an innovative training system for soccer players worldwide.

Emile M'Bouh M'Bouh was an important part of the Cameroon side in both the 1990 and 1994 World Cups, including playing in arguably the World Cup's biggest ever shock when they beat champions Argentina. He currently resides in the United States where he runs his own coaching academy; the Emile M'Bouh Soccer Academy, and the Lions Soccer Program in Montgomery.

Peter Mellor is an English ex-professional goalkeeper and has played just under 500 games in the top two divisions of England, including the 1975 FA Cup Final. Peter moved to the United States and has worked with the U.S. National Team at all levels in a coaching role. He currently works for the United Soccer Leagues as National Technical Director.

Shep Messing is a retired American goalkeeper, broadcaster, and TV personality. He played in the North American Soccer League and the Major Indoor Soccer League. He is a Harvard graduate and was a member of the U.S. soccer team at the 1972 Summer Olympics. He works in television and radio, including as a broadcaster for ESPN.

Rachel Nuzzolese was a vital member of the Wake Forest women's soccer team, which saw her named to the Atlantic Coast Conference tournament team twice. She went on to represent the U.S. Women's National Team at the U17 level, scoring a hat trick against El Salvador in a World Cup qualifier. She won a gold medal for winning their bracket.

John Pantsil is a member of the Ghana National Football Team and has eighty-eight caps to date. He has played his club football in a number of leagues, including almost a hundred games in the English Premier League. John is the founder of his own charity, Pantsil Peace Kids Project (PPKP), which works with children aged 8 to 12, teaching them peace, discipline, respect, tolerance, love, and unity.

Mark Patterson used to follow the Republic of Ireland across the globe, in tournaments and qualifying matches. He doesn't manage to get to as many matches as he would like now, but when he is in London for work, he tries to follow Arsenal as much as he can. He works for Global Benefits Europe B.V. Mark resides in North County Dublin with his wife, Clodagh. He has two grown children, Mark Junior and Kate.

Christopher Sullivan won nineteen caps for the U.S. National Team between 1987 and 1992, and scored two goals. He was a member of the U.S. team that competed in the 1990 World Cup in Italy. He has become one of the most recognizable soccer faces on American television due to his work for Fox Soccer, covering both international soccer as well as the MLS.

Kim Tate is a freelance sports writer and *The Telegraph's* Costa Rica correspondent at the 2014 World Cup in Brazil. She is also the owner of Kim Tate Sports. Kim has had numerous work published at Football. com, where she worked as a correspondent for U.S. and Mexican soccer.

Ian Thomson is an author of soccer books, such as *Summer of 67: Flower Power, Race Riots, Vietnam and the Greatest Soccer Final Played on American Soil*. A former Wall Street reporter, covering the stock market and corporate news for Dow Jones Newswires/*The Wall Street Journal* and Bloomberg News. Ian is also a contributor to *The New York Times* soccer blog, "Letter from America." Ian has had work published by the *New York Daily News*, *Houston Chronicle*, *GlobalPost*, *Scottish Daily Express*, and *Press and Journal*.

Nick Webster was a very familiar face on Fox Soccer where he worked for twelve years as a broadcaster, senior producer, director, and writer. He has covered three World Cups, in 2002, 2006, and 2010. Nick worked for Football.com as Director of Content and Development before becoming the Managing Director at RealFootyTalk.com. He is also the head coach at Windward High School in Los Angeles.

About
CertainRate Inc.

CertainRate Inc. is a privately held New York corporation with headquarters in Cazenovia, NY. It creates and distributes insurance products for Lloyd's of London and Willis Faber. The company provides consumers with affordable, guaranteed financial and health insurance products. Through CertainRate.com, online visitors are able to search annuity rates, fixed index annuities, multi-year guaranteed annuities, fixed index accounts and fixed annuities. The veterans involved with the company have originated bank product and corporate liability funding with many major banks. They are responsible for many innovative insurance products in the past 40 years. The company's current team includes Eric Weber, Tom Georgiadis, Darrin Carroll, and John Lofaro from Syracuse, NY. John Schoeninger and James Breck from Connecticut have been on the team for 25 years. CPA John Wolle and authors Mark Victor Hansen and Dr. Jerome Corsi and health insurance expert Lee Gerber complete the nucleus of the team. The company is also sponsoring the creation and distribution of a Chicken Soup for the Soul soccer book series.

James Griffin, CEO of CertainRate Inc., is an insurance executive from Cazenovia, NY and Singer Island, FL. He has been responsible for creating innovative new products and working with insurance companies, banks and brokerage firms for over 40 years. Mr. Griffin lives in Cazenovia, NY with his wife and has two adult children. He is a graduate of Long Island University, and holds a degree in Business. His wife Chary Griffin is on the USA Triathlon team, competing in the 2014 world championship in Edmonton, Alberta. His son James received a PhD from a joint program between Rand Corporation and the University of California in Environmental Economics and works for the State of Hawaii. His other son Michael played varsity soccer and graduated from Le Moyne College.

About Atlantic Sports and Performance

Atlantic Sports and Performance (atlanticsportsandperformance.com) is a sports specialist organization based in New York. It focuses on developing athletes of all standards to reach their highest potential through various coaching techniques and methods. Its work with boys and girls soccer teams on Long Island, NY has proven to be one of the most successful in New York. ASAP staff have over 30 years of experience worldwide in sports coaching, business and marketing. Atlantic Sports and Performance used their substantial expertise and contacts to produce this book.

Leigh Pilkington is President and owner of Atlantic Sports and Performance, CEO of Regal Sporting Group, and General Manager of US Operations for Club Atlético Boca Juniors (CABJ). Leigh is a soccer market specialist and has over 20 years of sports business experience worldwide. Amongst his impressive portfolio, he has worked with the following professional soccer organizations: The English Football Association, Chelsea FC, Liverpool FC, Celtic FC, FC Bayern Munich, FC Inter Milan, Reggina Calcio and D.C. United. Leigh attended Manchester University, graduating in Marketing and Management and holds additional degrees in Sports Development and as a Fitness Specialist.

Chris Leaver is the General Manager at Atlantic Sports and Performance as well as the Head of National and International Strategy at Regal Sporting Group. Originally from London, Chris achieved his bachelor's degree in his home city before moving to New York on a soccer scholarship to study for his master's degree. He graduated from Long Island University, where he captained the men's soccer team that is currently ranked third nationally. He has nine years of sales, marketing and business experience from both the UK and America, specializing in sport. Throughout his career, Chris has worked with some of the biggest names in world sport on various ventures.

Chicken Soup
for the Soul

www.chickensoup.com